T0122028

Biblical Truths
from
Uncle Otto's Farm

CHAIM BENTORAH

WESTBOW
PRESS
A DIVISION OF THOMAS NELSON

WestBow Press books may be ordered through booksellers or by contacting:

WestBow Press
A Division of Thomas Nelson
1663 Liberty Drive
Bloomington, IN 47403
www.westbowpress.com
1-(866) 928-1240

ISBN: 978-1-4497-6168-4 (sc)
ISBN: 978-1-4497-6170-7 (hc)
ISBN: 978-1-4497-6169-1 (e)

Library of Congress Control Number: 2012913695

Printed in the United States of America

WestBow Press rev. date: 08/13/2012

To My Niece, Nicole Ann

You had a great-great-uncle named Otto, who owned a little farm in Missouri. He had many animals on this farm, including a horse named King, a cow named Baby Doll, and a dog named Buddy. They all have stories to tell, stories that will delight all the little girls and boys who will bear the family name. You are the first of a new generation to bear that name. You are also the first who never had the opportunity to meet your great-great-uncle. May this book help to keep the memory of our uncle Otto alive for all our future generations.

Your uncle Chaim Bentorah

Contents

Introduction

GROWING UP IN the city, my only real encounter with animals was mostly as pets. When I first visited my great-uncle Otto's farm, I was awestruck not just by the number of animals but by the variety. I remember walking around the farm, just feeling the energy of the life that surrounded me.

Coming from a strong religious home, I knew and believed God created each one of these animals for a purpose, and at a young age, I was convinced that purpose was more than just to serve the physical needs of man. It was also to give us a glimpse into the nature and beauty of God. As a child, I felt each animal was speaking things about God that we, as humans, could not comprehend, but they, as animals, knew, understood, and were trying to communicate to us.

I never really lost this childish idea, and I still carry my childhood fantasy that when I ask an animal to tell me about God, they send a little message. I remember a time I was visiting a local shopping mall, which was hosting the 4-H Club. In the center of the mall was an area that was surrounded by a four-foot high fence. A large crowd of adults and children were gathered around this fenced-off area. Peering over the crowd, I saw two little lambs, quietly standing in the center of the pen. Children hung over the fence, throwing hay at the two animals, shouting at them, begging these two little creatures to come to them. Yet neither animal moved nor even looked in their direction. As I finally made my way to the fence, I placed my hands over the rail, looked at the two little lambs, and quietly began to sing my "Spirit Song," which I learned many years earlier on Uncle Otto's farm. Suddenly, the two lambs looked in my direction. The crowd started to grow quiet, because the lambs had suddenly acted like they were aware of the presence of the people around them. Then the crowd became silent as the two lambs slowly walked in my direction. I was conscious of the fact that everyone was looking at me, but I just kept silently singing my "Spirit Song," urging the two little lambs to teach me something about our Creator. As they came up to me, they pressed their noses against my hands, as if to say, "Our Creator is a gentle God." People turned to me, asking questions about the lambs, as they thought I was their owner. I thought about telling them what I was doing, but I figured, *What's the use?* This was just a moment I was sharing with the God I loved, who was sending His message of love to me through those two little lambs.

As an adult, I paid my way through college working as a ventriloquist, performing for many children's groups. Thinking over the purpose and goal I wished to accomplish in my performances, I knew I wanted to tell the children and adults about the nature and beauty of God. I figured that the best way to do this was to let the animals from Uncle Otto's farm teach these lessons.

CHAPTER 1

Baby Doll

UNCLE OTTO FINALLY retired to a little farm. This was his lifelong dream. He just loved to get on his tractor with his shirt off and let the hot sun burn his skin. Someone once commented that Old Otto ought to just sit back, relax, and enjoy his retirement. Aunt Ruth looked out into the field where Uncle Otto was working and said, "He is."

Uncle Otto had many different farm animals, including goats, sheep, cows, and his favorite, a beautiful white stallion named King. You see, one line on Uncle Otto's résumé said that he was once a cowboy. Grandpa used to say, "Otto really knew how to punch a cow." And this brings me to my story.

When I was about seven years old, we were visiting Uncle Otto. He had just retired and purchased this farm. My younger brother, who was about two years old, and I had wandered off into Uncle Otto's pasture and turned into a wooded area, where we heard a rustling noise. As we walked deeper into the woods, we came face-to-face with a monster that was headed right toward us!

Now you have to remember I was just a city boy, so I had never met a real, live cow face-to-face. My father was a milkman and I knew about cows, but I had no idea they were so big. And here was the biggest, meanest-looking cow coming to eat me up! I wasn't worried about my little brother, because I knew the cow would not eat him. He was too spoiled. But I knew she had her eye on me and was going to get her revenge for all those hamburgers I had eaten. I was so terrified I just froze, unable to run.

Then I heard a noise behind me. Uncle Otto was galloping up on King. Uncle Otto immediately appraised the situation, jumped off King, and calmly walked up to this monster that meant to harm me. Grabbing the cow by the head, he playfully twisted her head, saying, "This is my little Baby Doll, ain't cha, honey? You're just my little Baby Doll." Old Baby Doll gave Uncle Otto a serene, affectionate "mooooo." After a few minutes, my brother and I walked up to Baby Doll and began to pet her while Uncle Otto continued to hold her head. Baby Doll again mooed, and I mooed, and then we all mooed.

When we face the terrors and difficulties in life and suddenly hear something behind us, it is Jesus riding up on His white horse. He jumps off, grabs that problem by the head, twists it, and says, "This is just my little baby doll, ain't cha, honey? You are just my little baby doll." Before long, we begin to "pet" our problem.

So the next time you confront a difficult problem, just say "moo."

CHAPTER 2

A Pig in the Sunshine

IF YOU WERE to visit Uncle Otto's farm, you would have been impressed by how well maintained it was. All the buildings were in good repair, the grass was mowed, and all was well tended, except for one small area—the pigpen. You see, grass never grows in a pigpen; in fact, even in the driest weather, the pen is still just one big mud puddle. The reason is because pigs love to roll in the mud and then just lie in the sunshine and let the mud bake on their backs.

Now the pigs were not the only ones who depended on the sunshine. King was well aware that all that grass, hay, and alfalfa that he ate would not be possible if it were not for the sunshine. The chickens knew to lay their eggs, and Baby Doll knew it was time to give milk when the sun came up. Yes indeed, all the animals knew the consequences of a morning when the sun did not rise. For this reason, they lived in mortal fear that Rooster, their sun prophet, would one day not crow. You see, every morning when Rooster crowed, the sun came up. Therefore, by animal logic, when Rooster crowed, the sun came up. Therefore, Rooster made the sun rise.

Let us jump to our story about Silvia the pig. Silvia was not as large as the other pigs, and she did not smell as foul as the other pigs. Worst of all, Silvia's oink was unlike the oink of the other pigs. It was sort of high-pitched and squeaky. Silvia just did not meet the criteria that would exalt a pig in pigdom. However, she loved to roll in the mud and let it bake on her back in the sunshine just as much as the other pigs. But alas, the other pigs paid Silvia no mind. She was often shunned to the remotest part of the pigpen, often in the shade, where there was little mud.

"Oh," bemoaned Silvia, "if only I could do something really great and important. Something that would make me special in the eyes of the other pigs."

Silvia dreamed of some great exploit, something heroic that would make all the pigs praise her and make Brenda the sow fawn over her. She might even give Silvia her spot in the muddiest, sunniest part of the mud puddle that Brenda reserved for her favorite pig.

One morning, Silvia watched Rooster as he crowed the sun up in the morning and began to think. Now remember, pigs are of such little brain that they often think things that seem strange to us who are of more brain. Silvia began wondering why the sun would listen only to Rooster and to no one else. Maybe it was his special voice! Maybe Silvia's strange oink—no, not just maybe but in *fact*—was not a curse but a gift. A gift to call up the sun every morning!

Oh my friends, when one creates a fantasy about oneself, before long he or she begins to believe that fantasy is real. Soon Silvia began to puff herself up and shared with the other chickens her new revelation about herself. She was indeed a sun prophet, ordained to oink the sun up in the morning. She was the prophet-in-waiting. So if Rooster ever failed to crow, Silvia, with her gifted oink, would call the sun up.

Of course all the other pigs laughed at and mocked Silvia. Even though pigs have little brain, they knew that Silvia had more bacon than pork.

But one morning the animals on Uncle Otto's farm faced their worst nightmare. Rooster had a bad cold and lost his voice. Instead of a bold, loud "cock-a-doodle-doo," all that came out was a pitifully weak and raspy "cock-a-doodle-doo."

"Oh," mooed Baby Doll. "The sun will not rise. How will I ever give my milk?"

"How will we know to lay our eggs?" clucked the chickens.

"I will have no hay," whinnied King.

Even Brenda the sow panicked. "My beautiful mudhole will not be soft and moist," she oinked mournfully.

"Quick!" said Baby Doll to Buddy the dog. "Go get Uncle Otto's cough medicine."

"I'm on it!" barked Buddy.

You see, Uncle Otto used to make his own cough medicine. The word about Uncle Otto's cough medicine was that it came from the same root as moonshine. But hey, it worked for Uncle Otto, so surely it would work for Rooster.

Rooster sipped Uncle Otto's cough medicine. It burned as it went down.

"That means it's working," snorted King hopefully.

"Yes," said the pigs. "It is burning away that nasty cold that keeps Rooster's cock-a-doodle-doo quiet."

However, Rooster did not look well after drinking Uncle Otto's cough medicine. In fact, he had trouble standing.

"Go head," Baby Doll encouraged Rooster. "Give it a try."

Rooster fluffed himself up, staggered a little, and belted out. "Cocka (hic) do (hic) adoooooooooooooooo!" Then he passed out cold.

"Oh," moaned the farm animals. "He will never call the sun up now. We are doomed. Doomed!"

Then in walked Silvia. "You need not fear, my friends, for I have been gifted with a special oink. I have studied oink in the best pigpens in the country, and I know how to call the sun up."

Well all the animals knew Silvia was never at any other pigpens, but this was not the time to argue. It was certainly worth a try. So they quickly led Silvia to Rooster's fence post and left her there to call up the sun. Each farm animal then took its usual morning position.

What have I done? thought Silvia. *What if the sun does not rise? Oh how the farm animals will laugh at me.* But she had no choice. Maybe this was her moment, her opportunity to prove to the other farm animals just how special she was. So she gave it her best oink with all her strength. "Oink-di-oink-oink!"

To everyone's amazement and relief, the sun came up, shining as brightly as ever.

"She did it! Silvia oinked the sun up!" All the farm animals cheered. They gathered around her, praising and honoring her as a truly gifted pig with a gifted oink. Silvia beamed.

Then Brenda Sow stepped forward. "Come, little Silvia. Come share my mud puddle with me in that nice hot sun you oinked up."

Silvia's dream had come true. That afternoon, when King and Baby Doll walked by the pigpen, they saw Silvia lying in the muddiest, sunniest part of the pigpen.

"Yes," said King, "Silvia is truly a pig in the sunshine."

Remember: We may accomplish great things for God, but it is through God's power, and His power alone, that we do so. "Not that we are adequate in ourselves to consider anything as coming from ourselves, but our adequacy is from God" (2 Corinthians 3:5 KJV).

CHAPTER 3

The Fence

UNCLE OTTO TOOK very good care of his farm animals. He would prepare a delightful breakfast of oats and hay for King and Benjamin Goat. He mixed a special chow that Baby Doll loved, and of course, he purchased only the best dog food for his hound dog, Buddy. Every morning the animals would go to the barn, where Uncle Otto laid out the delights for his beloved animals.

One morning as the animals came to the barn they were confronted by a big fence.

"Say what?" asked King.

"Never saw this before," announced Baby Doll.

"What is it?" questioned Benjamin Goat.

"It's called a fence," said Buddy, who was pawing a metal plate on the fence that had some words on it.

Every night Buddy lay by Uncle Otto's stuffed chair as Uncle Otto read from his Bible. So Buddy knew something of words, and he was eyeing the words on the metal plate.

"What does it say, Buddy?" asked King.

"I think I recognize one of the words from Uncle Otto's Bible," said Buddy thoughtfully. "Let's see, g-i-l-t. But I don't recognize the rest of the words. Must be saying something like fencing."

G-i-l-t, thought King.

"Gilt; it must be the name of the fence," suggested Benjamin Goat.

"I don't care what its name is," spoke up Baby Doll. "All I know is that it is keeping me from my chow."

"You're right, Baby Doll," snorted King. "We need to get past this fence to get our breakfast. There must be an end to this fence. I will gallop along this fence and find a place to go around it so we can enjoy Uncle Otto's delights."

So King started off to his right in a gallop, but in a few moments, he approached from the left in a slow trot, shaking his head. He simply said that there was no way to go around the fence.

"Well," announced Baby Doll, "we will just have to go through it."

Taking her powerful body, she slammed it against the fence, but it did not move. She did it again and again.

Finally King shouted, "Woo, woo there gal. Give it up. That fence is not going to come down."

"I suppose you're right," Baby Doll said sadly as she nursed her bruised shoulder.

"Well we can't go around the wall," King sadly said.

"We can't go through it," said Baby Doll, rolling her bruised shoulder in some mud.

"But," announced Benjamin Goat, "we can go over it."

Now Benjamin Goat was always bragging how he was descended from a line of mountain goats. Here was his chance to prove it. Getting a running start, Benjamin Goat gave a mighty leap and slammed headfirst into the wall. He tried again and again and again. We all know what hard head goats have, and Benjamin most likely had the hardest head of all. It took almost ten attempts before he would finally admit that he could not jump over the wall.

"Well," King said, "we can't get around gilt."

"We can't go through gilt," injected Baby Doll.

"And we can't go over gilt," Benjamin Goat sadly admitted.

"I guess that leaves only one other way," Buddy said quietly. "Uncle Otto gets pretty mad at me when I dig holes, but this is an emergency. He will just have to forgive me. I'll dig a hole, and we will go under gilt."

So Buddy started to dig and dig and dig. Finally, an exhausted Buddy had to admit that they would not be able to go under the fence. The fence was buried too deep in the ground, and he could not dig deep enough.

As all the animals pondered the reality that they would not be able to go around gilt, or through gilt, or over gilt, or under gilt, they heard a noise in the distance.

King looked up and said, "It's Uncle Otto in that tractor thing." King was very jealous of the tractor; it seemed Uncle Otto rode it more than him.

"Maybe he has the Charles wagon hooked up to it," spoke up Baby Doll hopefully.

"That's chuck wagon, and I should know," said King jealously. "I used to pull it for Uncle Otto before he got that tractor thing."

"Nope, no wagon," declared Buddy, who had jumped up on a woodpile to get a better look.

Before long Uncle Otto arrived. He jumped off the tractor and said, "Well, well. I see my friends are hungry this morning."

Uncle Otto walked up to the fence. As Baby Doll affectionately nuzzled Uncle Otto, she noticed he pulled a little piece of brass from his pocket and shoved it into a bigger piece of brass connected to a chain. Suddenly, the chain fell, and a gate swung open. All the animals immediately went through the gate and into the barn, where they began to enjoy the delights and pleasures that Uncle Otto prepared for them.

> Romans 8:1: "There is now no condemnation to them which are in Christ Jesus."

We are all sinners, and it is the guilt of our sins that keeps us from enjoying all the things that God wants to give to us. We cannot go through that fence of guilt, around it, over it, or under it. Only Jesus can open the gate, forgive our sins, and remove the guilt so we can enjoy all the things that God has prepared for us.

The Chicken Who Could Fly

King, Baby Doll, and Buddy (Uncle Otto's hound dog) were having a bull session with Jezebel Chicken when King looked up and saw a beautiful bird soar through the air.

"Why look at that," shouted King in awe.

"Oh it is so beautiful," mooed Baby Doll.

"You know what type of bird it is?" Buddy asked, looking at Jezebel

You see, Jezebel was no ordinary chicken, as chickens go. She was very intelligent, clever, and ingenious.

"That is a red-tail hawk," Jezebel boastfully clucked with pride.

King, Baby Doll, and Buddy just looked at Jezebel with awe.

"Jezee," mooed Baby Doll, "you are very intelligent, clever, and ingenious, as chickens go." Jezebel just beamed with pride.

"Well," snorted King, "if you are so smart, why don't you fly? You have wings."

"We chickens may have wings, but we are not a-e-r-o-d-y-n-a-m-i-c-a-l-l-y designed to fly," Jezebel said as she fluffed herself up with pride.

"Whoa, wee," whinnied Buddy. "Jezee, you do have big words. You are intelligent, clever, and ingenious, as chickens go."

But as the trio walked away, Jezebel thought about this matter. She had wings, so why could she not fly? Maybe no chicken ever thought about it. But she was no ordinary chicken. Jezebel was very intelligent, clever, and ingenious, as chickens go. She thought on this and figured the reason she did not fly was because she never tried. Maybe if she got on the roof of the chicken coop and jumped off, this would give her the opportunity to spread her winds and fly.

So she climbed up on the roof, looked down at the ground, and seeing how far down it was, she almost backed out. However, she reminded herself that she was very intelligent, clever, and ingenious, as chickens go, and if she actually flew, oh how the animals would be impressed.

She jumped off the roof, flapped her wings, and fell to the ground like the proverbial rock. Alas, she did not fly.

But did I tell you, Jezebel was no ordinary chicken? She was intelligent, clever, and very ingenious, as chickens go. So she thought this out and figured that what she needed was a running start. So she climbed back onto the roof of the chicken coop, went to one end of the roof, and ran all the way across the roof as fast as she could, until she went over the side of the roof and straight down to the ground. Wooo, that hurt!

Suddenly, Crow flew up and asked Jezebel what she was trying to do. Jezebel said she was trying to fly like crow. At that moment, Jezebel had an inspiration. For did I fail to mention that Jezebel was no ordinary chicken? She was very intelligent, clever, and ingenious, as chickens go. She asked crow to get a friend and meet her back at the chicken coop in five minutes. She knew now that she was going to fly.

When crow returned with a friend, Jezebel had a long stick on the ground. She instructed crow to grab one end of the stick and his friend grab the other end, and she would cling by her beak to the middle of the stick. When the crows took off in flight, she would go with them, spread her wings, and actually fly. The crows looked at each other and both said, "Why chicken, that is the cleverest contraption we have even seen. You are truly intelligent, clever, and ingenious, as chickens go." Jezebel just beamed with pride.

So they took off on a test flight. Crow held one end of the stick, and his friend held the other. Jezebel clung to the middle of the stick with her beak. It worked perfectly, and when Jezebel spread her wings, it was like she was actually flying.

About this time, Uncle Otto was riding King in the pasture. He looked up, and there he saw one of his chickens flying through the air. No, there were two crows hanging onto a stick, and his chicken was clinging to the middle of the stick by her beak. It sure nuf did look as if she were flying.

Uncle Otto was so impressed he said, "King, would you look at that. You would almost think that chicken was flying. Who was the intelligent, clever, and ingenious individual who created such a contraption?" When Jezebel heard this, she beamed with pride, but fearing King or the crows would take the credit, she shouted out, "I was!"

Proverbs 16:18: Pride goes before destruction, a haughty spirit before a fall.

If we could trace our fall and failure to one single source, it would be pride and a haughty spirit.

When Buddy Wanted to Be a Wolf

Wolves no longer roam in what remains of Uncle Otto's farm today, but many years ago, there were packs of wolves that would invade the farm. Uncle Otto would pick up his rifle on many occasions, mount King, and go wolf hunting

"What's the matter?" asked Baby Doll to Buddy, who was just lying down and whining.

"Oh," replied Buddy, "Uncle Otto and King went off hunting for wolves, and again, Uncle Otto left me behind. I always go with Uncle Otto when he goes on his hunting trips, but he will not let me go when he hunts for wolves."

"Buddy, Buddy," snorted Pig, "you know why Uncle Otto leaves you behind. You would be no match for a wolf."

"You must understand," mooed Baby Doll, "Uncle Otto only wants to protect you.

At that moment, Uncle Otto and King returned.

"It's Uncle Otto and King," shouted Benjamin Goat excitedly. "I wonder if they found the wolves?"

After Uncle Otto unsaddled King, King came over to his friends.

"Any luck finding the wolves?" asked Pig.

"No," sighed King. "Wolves are very illusive. If we could only know their plans, we might trap them, but how to know?"

"The only way to do that is to be friends with a wolf," suggested Baby Doll.

"Not much chance of that," assured Buddy. "Wolves do not make friends."

"But Buddy does," spoke up Benjamin Goat excitedly. "What if we made Buddy into a wolf? Then he could go among them and learn all their plans."

"That is a great idea," said King,"

"Super idea," barked Buddy, suddenly coming alive at the thought of becoming a wolf. "Then I could join Uncle Otto on his wolf hunts and help him find the wolves."

All five friends agreed that Benjamin Goat's idea was brilliant. But there did remain the question of how they were going to change Buddy, a hound dog, into a wolf.

"Listen," whispered Pig. "You hear that off in the distance? That is the wolf howl. I live right next to chickens, and whenever they hear the wolves howl, they all run in fear for the chicken house. Now that is what Buddy needs to do; he needs to howl like a wolf, and when he does, that will make him a wolf."

"Okay Buddy," said Baby Doll, "let's hear it. Give us your best wolf howl."

"I ah woo woo!" howled Buddy.

"Needs work, Buddy," said King. "You know that it needs work."

"I'll work on it day and night if it will make me a wolf," assured Buddy.

So sure enough, hour after hour, day after day, Buddy practiced his wolf howl.

After some time, the friends gathered together again to see how Buddy was coming with his howl. This time when Buddy turned his head to the sky and opened his mouth, they heard a beautiful "ARF, ARF EEEEWHOOOOOO!"

"By George, you've got it," shouted King.

"You sound just like a wolf," mooed Baby Doll excitedly.

"He is a wolf," assured Benjamin Goat.

"Go," urged Pig. "Go to the chicken coop, give the wolf howl, and watch them run."

Buddy, filled with confidence, made his way to the chicken coop and let out his best "ARF, ARF, EEEEWHOOOO!" But the chickens did not run. In fact, all they did was look mournfully at Buddy.

Buddy overheard one say, "Poor Buddy, he must have gotten into Uncle Otto's cough syrup again, and now he has a stomachache."

Buddy was crestfallen.

Making his way back to his friends, he just shook his head and said, "I guess I cannot be a wolf by just howling like one."

"The problem," pondered Baby Doll, "is that you still look like Buddy. You do not look like a wolf."

"That's it," said King, getting excited again. "Remember that wolf Uncle Otto shot last year? He took the skin and turned it into a rug. Buddy, go and get that rug, and bring it here."

Buddy, knowing what King had in mind, quickly ran and retrieved the wolf rug.

"I get it," said Baby Doll. "If we put this wolfskin on Buddy, that will make him a wolf."

"Yes, yes," shouted Pig. "That will surely turn Buddy into a real wolf."

Then the four friends fastened and tied the wolfskin onto Buddy.

When they finished, they stood back and looked at their creation. "Why, I do say that is a wolf," said Benjamin Goat.

"He would fool me," grunted Pig.

"Go ahead, Buddy. Go to the chicken coop and give it a try," said King.

So Buddy went back to the chicken coop dressed like a wolf and gave another "ARF, ARF, EEEEWHOOOO!"

But instead of the chickens running away, they gathered closer to Buddy. and he heard them say, "Come, come everyone. Look at Buddy's Halloween costume."

Poor Buddy. That just hurt his little doggy feelings.

He walked back to his friends, really discouraged. He could not be a wolf by howling like one or by dressing like one. It seemed hopeless until King suddenly had an inspiration.

"Buddy, you are not a wolf because you do not belong to a wolf pack. If you belong to a pack, you will truly be a wolf."

"But I have no membership card," said Buddy thoughtfully.

"Doesn't matter," said Benjamin Goat with confidence. "Wolves come and go in packs. Just join up with them in your wolfskin, give that convincing howl, and you will be a wolf."

Buddy's friends had him convinced. So after they tightened up his wolfskin, Buddy gave his wolf howl and took off to find the wolves and join their pack.

Buddy went to Uncle Otto's pond, where he knew the wolves often hung out. Sure enough, they were there, waiting for some victim to come and get a drink of water. Buddy let out his wolf howl and boldly approached the wolves. The wolves suddenly formed a circle around Buddy and started growling menacingly. Buddy let out a growl, but it fell weak when he heard one wolf say, "Why if it isn't Buddy, Uncle Otto's hound dog. Uncle Otto shot one of our pack members last year. I say it is payback time."

"Payback time," growled the other wolves.

Buddy let out a "Gulp."

Suddenly, two shots rang out, and two wolves fell as the others scattered. It was Uncle Otto on King. He pointed his rifle at Buddy and just as quickly, lowered it.

"Is that you, Buddy?" asked Uncle Otto. "How did you manage to get tangled up in that wolfskin? Well King, it looks like Buddy has helped us drop two more of the enemy. Come on home, Buddy. You deserve a special treat, and from now on, you will join us on our wolf hunts."

As the trio made their way back to the farm, King whispered to Buddy, "We were wrong, Buddy. Uncle Otto does not need a wolf by his side; he just needs a hound dog."

"Yes," sighed Buddy. "But I sure would have loved to be a wolf."

"Buddy," replied King, who was now much wiser, "you cannot be a wolf by talking like a wolf, dressing like a wolf, or living with wolves. You can only be a wolf by being born a wolf."

> John 3:3: "Jesus answered and said unto him, Verily, verily, I say unto you, except a man be born again he can not see the kingdom of God."

We cannot become a Christian by talking like a Christian, dressing like a Christian, or going to church like Christians. We can only become a Christian by being born a Christian. When we accept Jesus Christ as our Savior, we will be born again, or born a Christian.

CHAPTER 6

The Sin of Buddy

It was a pleasant evening, and Buddy had just returned with Uncle Otto from a hunting trip. Buddy was very hungry, as was Uncle Otto. Aunt Ruth had already cooked Uncle Otto's dinner but had not yet laid out Buddy's bowl of dog food. Buddy lay by Uncle Otto's feet at the dinner table, waiting for Aunt Ruth to put out his bowl of dog food.

Aunt Ruth seemed unusually concerned about Uncle Otto, so much so that she forgot to lay out Buddy's dinner. And Uncle Otto seemed to also be preoccupied and failed to remind Aunt Ruth to put out Buddy's dinner. Poor Buddy. He just lay at Uncle Otto's feet, hoping Uncle Otto would cut off a piece of that nice juicy steak he was eating and give it to him.

Uncle Otto, however, was not eating. He just picked at his food and then stood up and said he was going to lie down. Aunt Ruth asked about the steak, and Uncle Otto said to give it to Buddy and went to his room. This got Buddy's attention, but Aunt Ruth did not give Buddy the steak. Instead, she followed Uncle Otto to the bedroom.

There was that nice juicy steak that Uncle Otto said he was to have, but Aunt Ruth was not there to give it to him. Buddy was hungry, and Uncle Otto did say to let him have the steak, so Buddy quickly grabbed it off Uncle Otto's plate and ran outside to his doghouse and started to chow down. As he was enjoying his steak, he looked up and saw King and Baby Doll glaring at him.

"What's wrong?" asked Buddy.

"Where did you get that steak from?" asked King.

Buddy told how he came about getting the steak for dinner.

"You mean Aunt Ruth did not give it to you?" asked Baby Doll.

"Well no, but Uncle Otto did say I should have it," responded Buddy defensively.

"Still, it was not given to you, and unless it is actually given to you, you stole it from Uncle Otto," snapped King.

"I did not. Uncle Otto said I should have it," barked Buddy.

"But it must be given to you, or it is still stealing," said Baby Doll firmly.

Poor Buddy. He was now feeling very guilty. He could not even finish the steak. Perhaps Uncle Otto did plan to eat the steak later. He could not return it now, as Uncle Otto could not eat it once Buddy had bitten into it.

"I just hope Uncle Otto does not get sick from not having his dinner, the dinner you stole from him, Buddy," said King worriedly.

It was late that evening when the flashing lights and bright headlights of a car/truck-looking vehicle drove up very quickly to Uncle Otto's farmhouse. In a few moments, men in white uniforms were carrying Uncle Otto out on a stretcher. He looked very pale and very sick. Aunt Ruth, in tears, followed.

King galloped up to the farm animals to announce that Uncle Otto might have had a heart attack.

"I knew it. I knew it," Baby Doll mooed mournfully.

"You see, Buddy," scolded King. "You see what happens when you steal from Uncle Otto? You stole his dinner, and now he is very, very sick. Shame on you, Buddy, shame."

All the other animals who knew of Buddy's sin began to join in on the chorus, chanting to Buddy, "Shame, shame, shame on you."

Poor Buddy went off by himself and began to whine. It was all his fault. He caused Uncle Otto to become very sick because he was so selfish. The next morning, there was a worried mood among all the animals about the fate of Uncle Otto. No one would talk to Buddy. No one would even come near Buddy.

"Bad doggy, bad," they said.

Buddy even overheard the chickens talking. Some were saying that Buddy snatched the steak right out of Uncles Otto's mouth and that he became sick when he started to chase Buddy to get it back. The sheep even began to talk about Uncle Otto getting sick because he was chasing Buddy. The pigs said Buddy had growled and actually bit Uncle Otto, and that was why he got sick.

That night, when Uncle Otto didn't return, the animals gather together, without Buddy of course, and began to talk.

"What do you think Uncle Otto will do with Buddy, if he returns?" asked Benjamin Goat.

"He will be sent to Uncle Claiborne's farm for sure," suggested Pig.

"Too good for him," said the chickens. "With the sins Buddy committed, he will surely be sent to the pound."

Poor Buddy. All he could do was just crawl under yon rock and cry. He had been a bad dog, and Uncle Otto would never forgive him.

The next day there was excitement on the farm. Aunt Ruth drove up in Uncle Otto's car, and who should step out but Uncle Otto. He was moving a little slowly, but he was smiling. He went into the house, and all the animals began to discuss whom Uncle Otto would greet first when he came into the barnyard.

"It will be King, of course," said the chickens.

"No, it will be Baby Doll," said Pig assuredly.

However, when Uncle Otto did come out, he walked straight to Buddy.

"Well that figures," said Benjamin Goat. "Uncle Otto needs to deal with that rubbish first."

But when Uncle Otto came up to Buddy, he gave Buddy a hug and began to pet him, saying things like, "Well, I had a little scare there. Thought I might not see my little friend again. Hope you enjoyed that steak. Good thing I didn't eat it. Doctor said it might have been harder on me if I did. And for just a little celebration of my homecoming, look what Aunt Ruth made for you."

Then Uncle Otto laid out a plate with a nice juicy steak.

"Eat well, my good and faithful servant," said Uncle Otto as he left to greet the other animals.

Romans 8:1: "There is therefore now no condemnation to them which are in Christ Jesus, who walk not after the flesh, but after the Spirit."

Others may condemn us for our failures and sins, but Jesus loved us and died for those sins and is always ready to forgive us for all our sins.

CHAPTER 7

King and the Mud Puddle

UNCLE OTTO HAD finished taking King for ride around the pasture, and King was feeling very joyful. Unfortunately for King, when he was feeling joyful, he would often throw caution to the wind. Such was this case as he trotted over to the chicken coop, adjacent to the pigpen. Now the pigpen is always muddy, and after a heavy rainfall, which had occurred just that morning, the mud gets very muddy and very deep. This can be very dangerous for a horse, and King should have known better, but he wanted to chat with chickens and share his joy. It was then that the worst happened.

King trotted right into the deepest mud puddle of all times. Immediately he sank up to his ankles. As he tried to pull out his hooves, the other hooves sank deeper.

"I'm stuck," King shouted.

Suddenly, all the chickens started squawking and the pigs started oinking. Now you must remember that pigs have little brain and chickens, by virtue of the size of their heads, have even smaller brain.

"You must pull yourself out," squawked chickens.

"Yes, you must pull yourself out," oinked Pig.

"But how?" whinnied King, who was now up to his shins in mud.

Pig thought on this a moment and then said excitedly, "King, you still have your harness on. Grasp your reins by your teeth and pull, King, pull."

"Yes, yes," the chickens started chattering. "You must pull yourself out. Pull on the reins, pull on the reins."

Well, poor King, who had more brain than the others, was just too frightened and desperate to use all his brain, and without thinking, he did as he was told to do and grabbed his reins by his teeth and began to pull.

"Pull, pull," chanted the chickens.

"You must pull harder. You must pull yourself out," oinked Pig excitedly.

Poor King. He pulled as hard as he could, but he only sank further. Now he was up to his knees in the mud puddle.

"I will be stuck forever," whinnied King.

Hearing the chickens squawking brought Buddy running to the chicken coop followed closely by Baby Doll.

When they saw what was happening, Baby Doll said, "Buddy, you must get Uncle Otto, quick."

"I'm on it," barked Buddy.

Buddy ran to the farmhouse and began scraping on Uncle Otto's door and using his best barking alarm. This brought Uncle Otto, who was eating lunch, right to the door.

"Hey Buddy, what's up?" asked Uncle Otto.

Uncle Otto then looked out toward the pigpen and saw the problem. "Come on, Buddy. We must hurry. Looks like King got himself stuck in the mud."

Uncle Otto went right to the barn, grabbed his rope, and ran to the pigpen.

On arriving, he looped the rope around King's head and said reassuringly, "Okay King, looks like it is my turn to pull on this rope. Just relax, old friend, and I'll have you out in no time."

Once Uncle Otto secured the rope, he began to pull. Baby Doll and Buddy each grabbed the rope by their teeth, and they too began to pull.

Slowly but most surely, King started to come out of the mud. Then, with a whooping cheer from all the farm animals, King was free.

> Ephesians 2:8–9: "For by grace are you saved through faith and that not of yourselves; it is a gift of God: Not of works, lest any should boast.

Just as King could not pull himself out of the mud, so, too, we cannot get to heaven by our own works. We can go to church, give our offerings, read our Bibles, and pray, but these things we do by ourselves will not get us to heaven any more than King pulling on his reins could get him out of the mud. Only Jesus can forgive our sins and take us to heaven.

CHAPTER 8

The Rope of King and Buddy

BUDDY TOOK HIS COMMISSION from Uncle Otto to protect the chickens in the chicken coop very seriously. I had never known Buddy to growl at me except when I got near the chicken coop and then all bets were off. You sure did not want to mess with Buddy when he was guarding Uncle Otto's chickens.

The chickens had many predators, but none were more threatening than Fox. Buddy had no fear of Fox, and woe to Fox if he got near the chicken coop. Buddy may have appeared to be an old, droopy hound dog, but if Fox threatened Uncle Otto's chickens, old Buddy would lay into him like ugly on an ape and chase him clear out of the county.

Foxes often hunt alone, but Buddy created a special circumstance such that Fox called his two cousins together to form an alliance and have it out with Buddy once and for all and put an end to Buddy's rule over the roost.

Fox met up with his cousins on Uncle Otto's land and they boldly walked into the area of the chicken coop where Buddy stood guard. As the foxes approached, Buddy immediately jumped up and began to give a fierce growl.

"Go ahead and growl, you old hound," said Fox insultingly. "You are barely a match for one of us, so you don't stand a chance with three."

"Let it be thirty," growled Buddy. "I'm ready. I'll take ya all on."

"Watch it," whispered King. "There are three of them, and they could do you harm."

"That is no concern to me," sneered Buddy. "I can handle 'em."

"You think so?" laughed Fox. "You're old, you're slow, and Uncle Otto only keeps you around out of pity."

"That's it," barked Buddy. "I've been itching for this fight. Let's have at it."

"Wooo, wooo," snorted King, using words that seemed to work well for him when Uncle Otto used them. "There will be no acts of violence on Uncle Otto's farm. Besides that, if Uncle Otto catches wind of a fight, he will be out here in an instant with his rifle, and he will have three new rugs to go with his wolfskin rug."

This had an effect on the foxes, and they backed off.

"Sure now," said Fox contritely, "we are reasonable foxes. Perhaps we can settle the score some other way."

"Perhaps," pondered King, winking at Baby Doll. "Let me get Uncle Otto's rope."

"Yes, yes," squawked the chickens. "There is magic in that rope."

You must understand that chickens are of little brain, and they tend to get superstitious.

"Yes, of course," snorted Pig. "I have also heard that if you say magic words over the rope, it will do wonders." Pigs have not much brain either.

"Well," said King, "we shall let the rope decide. What say you, foxes?"

"Agreed," responded the foxes. "We will let the rope decide."

With that, King went into the barn and dragged out Uncle Otto's long rope, which he used to pull up tree stumps. King pulled it over a large mud puddle and laid one end at the feet of the foxes. The other end was still in the barn, but King instructed Buddy to pick up the rope in the middle. With the foxes on one side of the mud puddle and Buddy on the other, King instructed the foxes and Buddy that at Baby Doll's signal, they were to pull the rope in a tug of war. The one who ended up in the mud would be the loser. The winner would have rule over the roost.

By this time, all the farm animals had gathered for the event. All were cheering for Buddy.

"Buddy is strong," said Alexander Goat. "His strength alone will make him the victor."

"No, no," cried the chickens. "It is the magic in the rope that will help Buddy win."

"The words," snorted Pig, "the magic words. We need the magic words."

"Baby Doll," said King, "if you feel Buddy is about to lose, you just moo out this battle cry: 'The rope of King and Buddy.'"

"Got it," responded Baby Doll with a mischievous grin.

So with great cheering and fanfare, Baby Doll gave the countdown: "3, 2, 1—pullllllllllll!!!!"

The challenge began. Buddy got in with a strong start, and the foxes quickly found themselves getting closer and closer to the mud. The farm animals went wild, snorting, grunting, squawking, and mooing with delight. But then Buddy began to tire. That was what the foxes had counted on. You see, foxes are very clever, and they deliberately let Buddy wear himself out while they saved their strength for one great pull.

Suddenly, Buddy found himself moving closer and closer to the mud.

"The magic words," cried Pig. "Baby Doll, say the magic words."

When it looked like Buddy was at the end of his rope, Baby Doll mooed as loudly as she could, "The rope of King and Buddy."

With that, Buddy gave a mighty pull on the rope with every ounce of strength he had. And a miracle occurred. Suddenly, Buddy was moving further and further away from the mud, and the foxes were moving closer and closer.

"The words, the words," screamed all the farm animals.

Again Baby Doll mooed as loudly as she could, "The rope of King and Buddy."

With that, Buddy used the last of his remaining strength for one final pull. The foxes flew into the air and landed in the mud. The whole farm erupted into cheers, and with renewed strength, Buddy gave a great growl and took chase after the foxes, chasing them clear into the next county, never to be heard from again.

A bitter dispute broke out among the farm animals.

"It was the magic of the rope," declared the chickens.

"No, it was the magic words," argued Pig.

"None of that superstitious stuff," announced Alexander Goat. "It was Buddy's strength."

"It was none of that," declared Baby Doll. "Buddy had a little help from a friend." With that, King walked outside of the barn, with the rope looped around his neck.

2 Corinthians 3:4–5: "And such confidence we have through Christ toward God. Not that we

are adequate in ourselves as considering anything as coming from ourselves, but our adequacy is from God."

Sometimes people will say good things about us. They will say we are very smart or very strong. They will say we worked very hard and accomplished some great deeds. Yet we must always remember that we have the help of a special friend to do the good things we do. His name is Jesus.

CHAPTER 9

Foxes Do Not Exist

CHICKEN WAS AGAIN eavesdropping on someone else's conversation. This time it was the conversation between King and Baby Doll.

"The water was extra cool and tasty this morning," snorted King.

"It is sure a hot day," sighed Baby Doll. "Oh but could I use a taste of that water. I think I will go there right away."

"There" was a spring-fed pond on Uncle Otto's farm that provided cool, clear springwater for all the animals on the farm. That is, of course, all the animals on the farm except for the chickens.

As Chicken listened to this conversation, it was more than she could handle.

"Sure now," she clucked to King and Baby Doll. "Look at you, free to move wherever you wish, free to go to the pond and drink that cool water while, we chickens are forced to drink tepid water here, because Uncle Otto keeps us cooped up in this, this, whatever it is."

"Coop," injected Buddy, who just joined the group. "Listen," said Buddy, "Uncle Otto does not keep you in this coop surrounded by, if you will pardon my language, chicken wire to imprison you. He is doing it to protect you."

"From what?" squawked Chicken.

"From Fox," said King.

"You see," said Buddy thoughtfully, "a fox is a distant relative of mine that looks a little like me."

"Only he has a long, pointed nose," added King.

"And they love to eat little chickens," injected Baby Doll.

"And Fox lives near the pond, which is why you cannot go to the pond," concluded Buddy.

"Oh come off it, guys. I wasn't born just last year, you know," shouted Chicken.

"Well, as a matter in fact—" Baby Doll was about to say something about Chicken's age, but she interrupted her.

"Look, you are just telling me this because you don't want me going to the pond. You are just saying this because you want all that cool water yourself."

"Chicken," said King gently, "we are your friends. We only tell you this because we care about you."

"Yeah, sure!" said Chicken angrily, now completely provoked. "You care by giving me some cock-a-doodle-do story about an animal that looks like Buddy and has a long nose and eats chickens? Foxes do not exist. I say."

With that, Chicken turned on her heels and marched off, repeating over and over, "Foxes do not exist. Foxes do not exist."

Buddy, King, and Baby Doll just sadly shook their heads, grateful that Uncle Otto cared enough to keep Chicken safe inside a chicken coop.

Later that day, Crow flew in for a visit with the chickens.

"Hey Crow," greeted Chicken. "Did you ever hear of an animal that looks a little like Buddy but has a long, pointed nose, lives near the pond, and eats chickens?"

Crow pondered this question for a moment and then responded, "Can't say I have, and I go to the pond every day. Who has been filling your mind with these fairy tales?"

"Oh my friends," squawked Chicken. "They came up to me and started to brag that they get to drink that nice cool water at the pond, while I have to drink the tepid water in this coop."

"Well that certainly does not sound like very good friends to me," said Crow self-righteously. "I will tell you something else about the pond. When the sun reflects off the pond, you can see your own reflection and see how beautiful you are."

This sure got Chicken's attention. She knew she was a sight to behold but had never seen herself. Why that explained everything. Her friends were jealous. They did not want her to see how beautiful she was, so they kept her from going to the pond. Why, any of them could pull back that chicken wire and release her to go to the pond. Would anyone do it? No. And why? Because they were jealous. That was why.

Seeing how impressed Chicken was with Crow's knowledge, he really got on his high branch and declared to Chicken that, indeed, foxes do not exist.

"Now you listen to me," declared Crow with a flourish. "First chance you get, go. Go to the pond, and drink that water. See your reflection and just how beautiful you are."

Well, Chicken did not have to wait long. That evening, a violent windstorm passed over Uncle Otto's farm, and among other things, it blew down the chicken wire. Chicken was the first to awaken, and when she saw the wire was down, she could not believe her luck. This was her chance, and she took it. She passed over the wire, out of the chicken coop, and headed in the direction she had seen King and Baby Doll go when they walked to the pond.

Now you can be sure it didn't take long for Chicken to arrive at the pond. Oh it was everything she dreamed it would be. Nice cool, clear springwater. And it tasted just oh so good. Then the sun hit the pond, and she saw her reflection. Yes, yes indeed, she was the most beautiful creature alive. For a moment, she felt a little forgiveness to her friends for keeping her from the pond, for they surely had reason to be jealous and not want her to see how beautiful she really was.

Now here comes the really sad part. If you are easy to tear up, you may want to reach for some Kleenex.

During this time of reflection, Chicken suddenly heard a voice behind her. "What do you think you are doing?"

She turned around, and there she saw an animal that looked a little like Buddy, but it had a long, pointed nose and was giving her a very evil look.

"Foxes do not exist. Foxes do not exist …" Chicken kept repeating those words as she moved back away from the animal.

"Foxes do not exist?" asked the evil intruder.

Her voice was getting weaker, but Chicken kept repeating, "Foxes do not exist. Foxes do not—"

Gulp! And Fox walked away, saying, "Chicken does not exist. Chicken does not exist."

> Proverbs 18:24: "A man that hath friends must show himself friendly: and there is a friend that sticketh closer than a brother."

Let it be understood that a crow will tell you what you want to hear, but a friend will tell you the truth. Your mother and father, your teachers, and your pastor are your best friends. They do not want you to get hurt, and when they tell you not to do something that you want to do, they are not being mean. They only want to protect you. But your best friend is Jesus, and the Bible will tell you what He wants you to do, so you do not get hurt.

CHAPTER 10

Buddy's Decision

WHACK! "YIP, YIP, yip, yip," cried Buddy. Grandma Ballard caught Buddy chasing rabbits in her garden once again, and poor Buddy paid for it with a whack on the head from Grandma Ballard's cane.

Grandma Ballard was in her nineties and often not of her usual mind. Aunt Ruth worried about her mother, and she and Uncle Otto invited her to live with them on the farm, so they could watch over her. This was a fine arrangement. She was really no trouble and spent most her time in a little garden that Uncle Otto provided. Grandma Ballard did not visit the animals much, and many were not even aware she lived on the farm. Actually, King, Baby Doll, Benjamin Goat, and Buddy were the only ones who had seen Grandma Ballard.

King would meet Grandma Ballard when Uncle Otto rode him up to the house, where she sat on the porch. She always had an apple ready to give to King.

For some reason, Grandma Ballard liked Baby Doll and would often come up to her to pet her and ring her bell.

Then, of course, Benjamin Goat was recruited to pull his cart, which Grandma Ballard filled with her tools and supplies to tend to her garden. I must tell you about Benjamin Goat's cart sometime.

Oh yes, and, of course, there was Buddy. Buddy was a house pet, and Grandma Ballard saw him more than any of the other animals. She did not seem to take a liking to Buddy. She often thought he was some wild animal, and when such a notion came into her head, she would sneak up to him and give him a whack on the head with her cane. Grandma Ballard could swing a mighty cane, and when it met with Buddy's head, he would scurry off with a "Yip, yip, yip, yip."

It didn't take too many whacks for Buddy to learn to keep his distance from Grandma Ballard. Sometimes, however, fate would rule out. This was particularly true when it came to Grandma Ballard's garden. Rabbits loved to feed in Grandma Ballard's garden, and Buddy loved to chase rabbits. Put the two together, and you had Buddy chasing a rabbit in Grandma Ballard's garden, pretty well tearing things up, until whack! "Yip, yip, yip, yip."

To create some peace between Buddy and Grandma Ballard, Uncle Otto installed a four-foot-high picket fence around the garden to keep Buddy out.

This worked fine until one day, Grandma Ballard got it into her head that she would take care of this wild animal once and for all. Now Grandma Ballard was not always the sky pilot she appeared to be. When she put her mind to it, she could be pretty discerning. She figured out a way to trap Buddy where she could give him one really good whack.

She found this large bone, still with some juicy meat on it. She carefully laid it by the fence inside the garden and then hid behind the huge oak tree in the center of the garden to wait.

Sure enough, Buddy smelled the meat on the bone and approached. That meaty bone looked so good he could almost taste it.

"Careful," said King. "You know what happens when you get close to Grandma Ballard's garden."

"Whack!" mooed Baby Doll in a moo version of whack.

"I just brought supplies in my wagon for Grandma Ballard," said Benjamin Goat. "She's around there somewhere and heavily armed with her cane."

Buddy didn't hear any warnings from his friends. He only had eyes for that meat bone. In a flash, Buddy pushed his head between the picket fence, grabbed the bone, and tried to pull his head back out of the fence. There was a serious problem, however. Now that he had the bone in his teeth, he could not pull his head and the bone out together. The only way to get his head out from between the fence slats was to drop the bone.

"Buddy," mooed Baby Doll in alarm, "you must let go of that bone." Oh but that bone with its meat tasted oh so good. Buddy just could not; he would not let it drop.

"Let it go. Drop it," cried Benjamin Goat. "Grandma Ballard and her cane are nearby. You must let go of it."

But Buddy could not let go of his prize. It was just too tasty, too wonderful to let go of. He wanted it; he wanted it oh so bad.

"Too late!" neighed King. "There's Grandma Ballard now, and she is waving her cane. Let go of the bone, Buddy. Let go of the bone. Just drop it."

"Wow," said Baby Doll. "That must be the new advanced model of a cane. I never saw one that big. Buddy, let go of that bone."

Buddy looked up and saw Grandma Ballard approaching with that mighty cane. The excitement of giving what she thought was a wild animal a good solid whack must have taken thirty years off her age, for she was approaching at a speed that would be difficult for a woman half her age.

Buddy looked up in terror, but he would not let go of that bone.

"Let go of it, Buddy. Let go of it," cried all his friends.

WHACK! "Yip, yip, yip, yip, yip!!"

> Philippians 3:13: "Brethren, I count not myself to have apprehended: but this one thing I do, forgetting those things which are behind and reaching forth unto those things which are before, I press toward the mark for the prize of the high calling of God in Christ Jesus."

There are some things that will come into our life that we just want so very much. Yet sometimes it may really bad for us, and Jesus tells us that we must let go of it, or it will eventually begin to hurt us and keep us from becoming the person that Jesus wants us to be.

CHAPTER 11

The Clover Patch

UNCLE OTTO HAD many acres of land for King to graze upon. Uncle Otto took very good care of his land and planted a variety of grass for King and his animals to eat. He also made sure that nothing harmful to his animals would grow on his land.

A fence divided Uncle Otto's land from his neighbor's land. The fence served to keep Uncle Otto's animals from wandering on his neighbor's property, which would be very impolite to his neighbor. The fence also kept Uncle Otto's animals from grazing on his neighbor's land, where things grew that were not healthy for his animals, such as clover.

Now clover is not good for horses, because it will give them gas and make their stomachs bloat. This can be fatal to a horse, as they do not have the resources to expel that gas like we or other animals can. So Uncle Otto took great care to keep King from eating any clover.

King, of course, did not understand this. So it happened one day, as King and Baby Doll were grazing, they wandered near the fence dividing Uncle Otto's and his neighbor's properties. King looked longingly at the neighbor's pasture, which was overgrown and quite ugly. To King, however, that only meant there was rich grazing with that long grass. Baby Doll walked up to the fence and began to stare at something.

"What's got your attention, Baby Doll?" questioned King.

"Come," said Baby Doll, "look at that strange grass. It is flat with little leaves."

King came closer and said, "I think I know what they call it. I heard Uncle Otto speak of it; I think he called it clover."

Clover? wondered Baby Doll. "Sounds tasty."

"Sounds tasty? It looks tasty," said King wistfully.

King stuck his head through the fence and could barely reach the clover, but he managed to get some. King was beside himself.

"Oh Baby Doll, that is the tastiest grass I have ever eaten. I cannot believe Uncle Otto will not let it grow on our side."

"Uncle Otto would if he didn't have a good reason not to," said Baby Doll wisely.

But King was so filled with temptation for the clover that he just did not have a lick of sense at that moment. All King knew was that he had to have some more clover.

All of a sudden, King said, "Yes, I remember! Just down a ways, a fence post is down. I can jump the fence there and come back for the clover."

"Whoa, whoa!" cautioned Baby Doll, using words that Uncle Otto used to stop King. "Now you know if Uncle Otto felt it was okay to eat clover, he would not hesitate to give it to you. You'd better think this over first."

But King paid no mind; he had to have that clover. King took off at a gallop toward the fallen fence post, and in a few minutes came trotting back to Baby Doll. Now on the other side of the fence, King wasted no time and began to devour the clover. *Oh how good it tasted. Surely Uncle Otto would not deny such a pleasure to his own horse,* thought King as he kept eating, eating, and eating. Baby Doll just watched, shaking her head.

After a season of feasting, King returned to the other side of the fence, where he and Baby Doll started back to the barn. Later that evening, after supper, Baby Doll returned to the barn to find out why King was not out for his evening run. Baby Doll found King, bracing himself against the wall of the barn.

"King, what's wrong?" asked Baby Doll.

"I don't think I feel so good," groaned King.

Baby Doll looked at King's stomach. It was swollen twice its normal size.

"Buddy, Buddy," cried Baby Doll. "King is real sick. You've got to get Uncle Otto."

Buddy came racing into the barn, took one look at King, and began to whine. "I'll get Uncle Otto," he barked.

Buddy raced to the farmhouse and scratched at the door. When Uncle Otto came to the door, Buddy jumped down and raced to the barn.

"Buddy," cried Uncle Otto, "what's wrong?" Uncle Otto grabbed his coat and raced out to the barn, where he found a very contrite and sick King.

"Oh King," cried Uncle Otto, "you've been eating that clover, haven't you? You're about to die, old buddy."

Uncle Otto then raced to the house and returned in a few minutes with a bottle filled with foaming white stuff. Uncle Otto tied King to his stall. He took that bottle filled with that horrid white stuff and began to force it down King's throat. Poor King. He could not understand why Uncle Otto was being so mean to him when he was so sick. Surely this was Uncle Otto's way of punishing him for eating the clover.

After forcing the liquid down King's throat, Uncle Otto patted him and said, "Now old friend, just rest. You will be fine."

And true to Uncle Otto's word, the next morning, King was his old self, but also much wiser. King no longer cared if the grass was greener on the other side of the fence.

Proverbs 14:12: "There is a way which seemeth right unto a man, but the end thereof are the ways of death."

In the Bible we find many things that God tells us not to do. He does not forbid us from doing these things just to be mean but to protect us. Some of these things may seem like fun and something we really want, but they could also be things that will hurt us later.

CHAPTER 12

Wolf Cookies

GRANDPA AND UNCLE Otto had once been sheepherders. They used to talk about something called "wolf cookies." A wolf seemed to know that they could not just run into a herd of sheep and grab what they wanted. The shepherd would shoot them with his rifle.

So the wolves knew that they had to sort of entice a sheep or a lamb to leave the fold and then they could attack. Grandpa and Uncle Otto used to call this enticement, "wolf cookies."

One day while Buddy and Uncle Otto were off on a hunt, Baby Doll sort of hung around close to the sheep. She had that bell around her neck, and if wolves showed up, she would start to ring it to send for Uncle Otto. It was not so much that sheep have little brain but that they were such trusting creatures, creatures of little discernment.

Well, Baby Doll was having a little chat with Naomi Lamb.

"Now you must beware of any wolves while Uncle Otto and Buddy are off hunting," warned Baby Doll.

"What they hunting for?" asked Naomi.

"Wolves, of course," mooed Baby Doll.

"Why would they want to hunt wolves?" asked Naomi.

"Why a wolf will come along and snatch any one of Uncle Otto's lambs or sheep and eat them up. That is why Buddy is always around and Uncle Otto carries his rifle."

"What does a wolf look like?" asked Naomi.

"Well," pondered Baby Doll, "a little like Buddy, but they are very fierce looking, with beady red eyes and big sharp teeth."

Naomi gasped. "I sure hope I do not meet up with one. They sound just too horrid."

Well later that day, as Baby Doll wandered back to the barn for her chow, Naomi looked after Baby Doll wonderingly.

"Sure nuf," stated Naomi to no one in particular, "that Baby Doll has it nice, getting a tasty mixture of chow while I just get to eat grass. I sure would love to try something different."

"Perhaps I can be of assistance," spoke a charming voice.

Naomi looked around, and there she saw an animal that looked a little like Buddy, but this animal had beady red eyes and sharp teeth."

"Oh mercy Maude," gulped Naomi. "You must be one of those simply horrid wolves Baby Doll warned me about."

"Horrid?" spoke the animal in a hurt voice. "Why should you say that. You have not even met me. Who is this Baby Doll that is filling your head with such ideas?"

"Why Baby Doll is my friend, and she warned me about you," affirmed Naomi.

"Oh I know about Baby Doll," said the wolf. "She eats a tasty chow while you sheep and lambs must eat just grass. And what kind of friend is this that would not share her chow with you? Why if you were my friend, I would share my wolf cookies with you."

"Wolf cookies?" Naomi bleated. "Oh but that sounds simply delightful. What do they taste like?"

"Like nothing you have ever tasted," affirmed the wolf enticingly. "Once more, I will share them with you, because I can be a much better friend than this Baby Doll. Come, my darling little friend. Come with me to the wolf cookie bar, and I shall bring you delights you could only dream of. You shan't allow these so-called friends to fill you with such horrid stories about me. They only want to keep you from enjoying the wolf cookies. Now let us be off."

Oh but what this evil wolf was plotting to do with our little Naomi, well such ears as yours should never hear. For once the wolf had little Naomi alone, his eyes got very red, and his teeth seemed to get sharper by the minute. Poor Naomi could only give a frightened little "baa."

"And now it is time for me to eat my little wolf cookie," said the wolf with a sinister snarl.

Suddenly, a shot rang out and then the fierce bark of Buddy followed, causing the wolf to leave his little wolf cookie and run off. Uncle Otto and Buddy were returning from their hunt when they heard Baby Doll's bell ringing. As Uncle Otto, King, Buddy, and Baby Doll approached, Naomi promised herself to always remember who her friends were and to never be tempted by wolf cookies again.

1 Peter 5:8: "Be sober, be vigilant; because you
adversary the devil, as a roaring lion, walketh
about, seeking whom he may devour."

There is a devil out there, and he will promise us many tasty treats and delights. We must listen to the warnings from our true friends and read our Bibles to know what Jesus, our best friend, tells us to do.

CHAPTER 13

Uncle Otto's New Animals

Uncle Otto would often purchase some of his animals from his brother-in-law, Uncle Claiborne. Uncle Claiborne had a much larger farm and actually used it to make a living, whereas Uncle Otto used his farm like a hobby. Well one day, Uncle Otto purchased a pig and a milk cow to add to his farm family. As always, Uncle Otto sent for the local vet to check out the new members of the farm family. Buddy, King, and Baby Doll were on hand to greet their new friends while they were in the holding pen, waiting for Doc's arrival.

"What do you think of our new friends?" asked Baby Doll.

"Well," said King, "I sense the heart of Milk Cow is sad and lonely. But the heart of Pig is most joyful with expectations."

You see, King had that rare gift of being able to read the heart of other animals.

"Well," barked Buddy, "it appears Pig is anxious to get our attention. Let's go over and introduce ourselves."

So they went over to Pig and made their introductions.

"Oh jolly," oinked Pig excitedly. "I have heard so much about Uncle Otto's farm. I am so happy to have been chosen to live here.

Tell me, my new friends, what is it really like on Uncle Otto's farm. What are the animals like? Are they all friendly, caring, and loving like I've heard?"

Knowing the heart of Pig, King answered her question with a question of his own. "Tell me, Pig, what was it like on Uncle Claiborne's farm. What were the animals like?"

"Oh, bacon and cheese," oinked Pig disgustedly and bitterly. "They were all selfish, self-centered, thinking only of themselves, caring only for themselves. I am, of course, not like that. I am a caring and compassionate pig, and no one appreciated me. That is why I am so glad to be on Uncle Otto's farm, for I know the animals here are different, and I shan't have any trouble at all fitting in."

"Oh my dear Pig," mooed Baby Doll, "I have lived on Uncle Otto's farm all my life, and it pains me to have to tell you that the animals on Uncle Otto's farm are no different than the ones you found on Uncle Claiborne's farm."

Aww, poor Pig, she looked so crestfallen. She had hoped to finally find a home where her talents and her compassionate and loving nature would finally be appreciated. All her hopes were dashed as she learned the animals on Uncle Otto's farm were just as unfriendly, uncaring, and unloving as those on Uncle Claiborne's farm.

Our friends left Pig to wallow in her muddy self-pity and walked over to the sad Milk Cow.

"Our dear new friend," whimpered Buddy, "do cheer up. Why are you so sad."

"Moo, sob, moo," replied Milk Cow. "How I miss Uncle Claiborne's farm. Oh what will I ever do? Tell me, my new friends, what are the animals like here on Uncle Otto's farm?"

Reading Milk Cow's heart, King wisely answered Milk Cow's question with a question. "What were the animals like on Uncle Claiborne's farm?"

With that question, Milk Cow's face, as cow faces go, brightened. A shinny countenance came over her as she said, "Oh the animals on Uncle Claiborne's farm were the friendliest, most caring, and most loving animals you would every want to meet. I know I shan't ever find animals with such compassion and love again. How my little cow heart breaks over having to leave them. Tell me, my new friends, what are the animals on Uncle Otto's farm like?"

With that, Baby Doll walked up to Milk Cow, sort of nuzzled her as cows often nuzzle each other, and whispered, "Milk Cow, the animals on Uncle Otto's farm are just like the animals on Uncle Claiborne's farm. Welcome home."

Matthew 7:4: "And why behold the speck in your brother's eye but you do not consider the board that is in your own eye?"

If you feel as if someone is unfriendly or mean to you, perhaps the first thing you should do is think about how you are acting. Maybe it is because you are being just as mean and unfriendly yourself.

CHAPTER 14

The Secret of Uncle Otto's Bell

WHEN UNCLE OTTO purchased his farm, there was an old dinner bell in the backyard. This bell was used in times past to call the menfolk in from the field and let them know that dinner was ready. I guess out of pure habit, Aunt Ruth would ring the bell to call Uncle Otto to lunch or dinner, and out of an equally pure habit, within minutes Uncle Otto would appear.

The animals were quick to learn that whenever that bell rang, Uncle Otto would suddenly appear as if out of nowhere. The animals may not have seen Uncle Otto all morning or afternoon, but once Aunt Ruth rang the bell, there was Uncle Otto.

The animals would often discuss the power that was in that bell to summon Uncle Otto.

"I can moo all day," said Baby Doll, "but it rarely brings Uncle Otto."

"Many times at night I would like a visit from Uncle Otto," barked Buddy. "I would bark and howl, and all I would get is a loud 'Shut up!' from Uncle Otto."

"Well, I would gallop and trot around the barn, hoping to bring Uncle Otto out for a ride, but he rarely showed up. And when he did, he would say 'Not now.'"

"Even Rooster's cock-a-doodle-doo does not bring Uncle Otto until at least an hour later," clucked Chicken.

"But that bell," they all said in unison.

"Yes," oinked pig, "there is indeed magic in that bell."

"Not magic," cooed Crow, "but a connection. That bell is in tune with Uncle Otto."

Well Crow's liberal, New-Age philosophy impressed no one. Especially Baby Doll, who pondered the theology of the bell and knew it had something to do with the number of rings and their noise level. All the other farm animals just accepted by faith that the way to summon the presence of Uncle Otto, the way to Uncle Otto's heart, was to ring the bell.

One day Aunt Ruth and Uncle Otto went to Uncle Claiborne's farm for a party, and Uncle Otto did not return for the usual 5:00 p.m. feeding of the animals. That sometimes happened, but Uncle Otto usually made it back within the hour to feed his animals. However, when 6:00 p.m. came and Uncle Otto was not there to feed them, the animals began to panic.

"The bell," mooed Baby Doll.

"Yes, there is magic in the bell to bring Uncle Otto," oinked Pig.

"King, you can reach the bell. Ring it, and bring Uncle Otto to feed us," clucked Chicken.

All the animals then approached the sanctuary of Uncle Otto's backyard. They rarely went to such a holy place, but this time it was an emergency; they needed to eat. King grabbed the cord to the bell and began to ring the bell fiercely. Uncle Otto did not appear.

"You must ring it gently, like Aunt Ruth does," mooed Baby Doll.

"Yes, the manner in which one rings the bell is important," said Crow, who arrived to add his two cents worth.

So King rang it gently. But Uncle Otto did not appear.

"Ring it three times," said Buddy. "That is what Aunt Ruth does."

King rang it three times, but still Uncle Otto did not appear.

At Baby Doll's suggestion, King tried to ring it three times in rapid succession and then did that three times. That still did not bring Uncle Otto.

It's the connection," squawked Crow.

"He's right," said Baby Doll thoughtfully. "Aunt Ruth rings it a way special for her. Perhaps you can ring it in the cadence of your trot when Uncle Otto rides you."

"Woo, that is deep," oinked Pig. "Do it, King. That will surely work."

So King gave the bell a slow, rhythmic ding a ding a ding. But Baby Doll's deep theology no more brought the presence of Uncle Otto than Crow's New-Age philosophy.

Finally, with one last yank, King gave the bell a solid, firm ring.

To everyone's surprise and relief, that actually did it. Uncle Otto came driving up the road with Aunt Ruth. All the animals rejoiced. They had discovered the secret of the bell to summon the presence of Uncle Otto. Now whenever they needed Uncle Otto's presence, all they had to do was give the bell one solid, firm ring.

And so it was that for months and even years later, the animals would give that bell a solid, firm ring to summon Uncle Otto. But he rarely came, and when he did show up, he did not seem too happy about the ringing bell. Still the animals would never lose faith in that old bell, and whenever they needed Uncle Otto's presence they, would give that bell a solid, firm ring. The rare times it worked was cause for some real testimonies among the animals and renewed faith in the secret of Uncle Otto's bell.

2 Corinthians 4:7: "But we have this treasure in earthen vessels, that the surpassing greatness may be of God and not of ourselves."

We do not have to go to church to find Jesus, read our Bibles to get His attention, or sing religious songs to bring Him to us. He is with us every moment and hour of the day.

CHAPTER 15

The Big Stink

BUDDY HAD MANY hobbies, but his most favorite hobby in the world was chasing cats. He just loved to approach a cat, give a "woof woof," and watch that cat take off running as he chased after it.

One day he noticed a new cat wander onto the farm, just as boldly as you please. Now such arrogance never set well with Buddy, and as we all know, cats can get pretty arrogant. But this cat was even more arrogant than most. So Buddy decided to let this new visitor know just where a cat stood on this farm.

Buddy approached this odd-looking cat. It was all black and had a white stripe down his back. Buddy sort of giggled to himself, thinking that he was going to turn that white stripe into a yellow stripe when he let out his first bark.

When Buddy got close enough, he let out his most fierce "woof woof."

But rather than this cat fleeing in terror, he just stood there and looked at Buddy as if to say, "Are you barking at me? Surely you could not be saying 'woof woof' to me."

Buddy gave a fierce growl and said, "Better watch it cat, or you're gonna drop from nine to eight lives."

The little catlike animal just turned up its nose and said, "My name is not Cat. It is Skunk, and when a skunk goes 'pssst,' hound dogs go 'Yip, yip, yip.'"

And with that, the skunk went "Pssst!"

The skunk sprayed Buddy with skunk stink, and Buddy went "Yip, yip, yip."

Oooo! Did that ever burn Buddy's eyes. He ran all the way back to his doghouse without taking a breath. As he lay in his doghouse, nursing the burning in his eyes, he began to smell something, something awful.

"Oh my," said Buddy. "This doghouse really stinks, stinks to high heaven."

He quickly ran from the doghouse to the chicken coop. Arriving at the chicken coop, he lay down to rest, glad to be out of that stinky doghouse. But as he lay in the chicken coop, he began to sniff the area, and there it was again, that hideous odor.

Buddy look around and sniffed again. "This chicken coop stinks. It stinks to high heaven."

Buddy took off running to the pigpen next door, hoping to find some relief from that awful stench.

Arriving at the pigpen, Buddy paused, sniffed the air, and declared, "This pigpen stinks, and it stinks to high heaven."

Buddy took off running to the barn. Entering the barn, he sniffed the air, and to his horror, there it was again, that awful odor.

"This barn stinks," announced Buddy, running from the barn to the cornfield.

In the middle of the cornfield, Buddy sniffed the air and whined, "This whole farm stinks."

Buddy ran off the farm and into the middle of the highway, sniffed the air, and howled, "The whole world stinks."

But you see, the world didn't stink. Buddy stank.

Matthew 7:3: "And why do you look at the speck in your brother's eye, but do not notice the log that is in your own eye?"

Before you say that someone else is at fault, look at yourself to be sure it is not you who are at fault.

CHAPTER 16

Good Dog

"That's it, Buddy, bring it over here. That's it. Good dog, good dog. Here's a Milk Bone," said Uncle Otto after Buddy returned the stick that Uncle Otto had tossed to him.

Buddy just beamed with joy. Uncle Otto said he was a "good dog." That was the word that Uncle Otto gave to Buddy, "good."

Buddy walked among his animal friends with his head held high.

"Well why are you looking so high and mighty today?" King asked.

"I just got a word from Uncle Otto," announced Buddy with pride. "He said I am a good dog."

"Hmmm," mooed Baby Doll. "I wonder what Uncle Otto meant by 'good'? Why did he not say you were the best or the greatest, and what does 'good' mean anyway?"

"Good?" clucked Chicken. "Seems to me Uncle Otto said that about our feed the other day. Yep, he said it was good feed. Uncle Otto must think you are not worth much more than chicken feed."

Buddy was thinking on that when Benjamin Goat offered his insight. "The other day after we had that terrible storm that did all that damage to our barn, Uncle Otto said, 'Yep, that was a pretty good storm, all right.' 'Good' must mean something that causes damage. Uncle Otto thinks you must do a lot of damage around here."

"Not only that," oinked Pig, offering her piglike insight, "Uncle Otto looked at us pigs just yesterday and said, 'These pigs are sure good and fat.' 'Good' must mean you are fat."

Buddy put his head down and gave a little whimper.

At this point, King joined in and offered, "Uncle Otto and I were trying to pull an old stump out of the ground, and it would not move. Finally, Uncle Otto said, 'That old stump is so stubborn, it is in the ground for good.' Uncle Otto was telling you that you are just stubborn."

Then Crow flew up and said, "Wait everyone, we need to look at the root meaning of the word 'good.' It has to do with something that is out of the ordinary. You see, Buddy, by using the word 'good,' Uncle Otto was trying to say there was something wrong with you. You are not an ordinary dog, you have—"

"Enough!" barked Buddy. "I don't care what your individual interpretation of the word 'good' is. I happen to know it means he really likes me."

"Like chicken feed?" questioned Chicken.

"He likes someone who does damage?" inquired Benjamin Goat.

"Or someone who is fat?" asked Pig.

"Or stubborn?" asked King.

"Yes," confirmed Crow. "Just how can calling you 'good' mean he likes you?"

"Because," barked Buddy, now well provoked, "I may not know what 'good' is, but I know Uncle Otto's voice, and his voice says I am something special."

John 10:26: "My sheep hear my voice and I know them, and they follow me."

When you read God's Word, you may feel as if God is speaking something special to you. Listen to His voice and not to the voice of others who put their own personal spin on that passage and make it sound as if it is something less that God is telling you.

CHAPTER 17

The Sunrise Service

BUDDY RAN INTO the farmyard with exciting news. He had just overheard that Uncle Otto was hosting the Easter sunrise service this year. The animals all gathered around, filled with excitement. "What is it all about?" "What is going to happen?" "Who is coming?"

"Settle down," barked Buddy, "and I will explain. Every year, Uncle Otto's Baptist church has a special service where they get up real early in the morning and go out to some special place to observe God's creation as the sun rises. Then they all get together to have breakfast and do those things that humans do."

"Breakfast?" mused Baby Doll. "I bet you Uncle Otto will come to us to make a contribution for this breakfast."

"We will sure be happy to contribute our eggs. Won't we gals?" clucked Chicken.

"All the eggs Uncle Otto needs," squawked the other chickens.

"Well, the other milk cows and I will provide all the milk that is needed," boasted Baby Doll. "We sure won't mind. Will we gals?"

All Uncle Otto's milk cows mooed in agreement.

"That is nothing," said Sheep, now pretty disgusted with all this boasting. "You think you are making such a contribution to this sunrise service. Well I will have you know the other sheep and I are going to get our summer crew cuts early, just so Uncle Otto can use our wool to make nice soft cushions for his guests to sit on while eating. Won't we gals? Let me tell you those church people would not enjoy your precious eggs or drink your milk if they did not have something comfortable to sit on, and we are giving up our winter coats for this occasion. So you top that, will you."

"You bet I can top that," snorted King. "Without me, this breakfast would not be possible."

"Now how do you figure that?" asked Buddy.

"Uncle Otto is going to bring the breakfast over in his Charles wagon, and he cannot pull that wagon without me." King stamped decidedly.

"That's *chuck* wagon," growled Buddy, now fully provoked by all this boasting and self-righteous satisfaction and everyone's smugness at their offerings beyond their tithe.

"Listen King," barked Buddy, "Uncle Otto could easily hitch up John Deere to that wagon, and that Johnny Deere could pull that wagon faster and better than you any day."

"Don't make me laugh," snorted King. "I saw and smelled that John Deere's smoky, oily fart. Uncle Otto would never allow that filth to cover his breakfast."

"Ha," clucked Chicken. "You're a fine one to talk about foul-smelling farts. Why last time you got into that clover patch, the whole farm almost—"

"Enough, enough," oinked Pig. "All of you, bragging about your little offerings. Well I've got news for you. You are only making a contribution. Me? I am making a sacrifice."

Romans 12:1: "I beseech you therefore, brethren, by the mercies of God, that you present your bodies a living sacrifice, holy acceptable unto God, which is your reasonable service."

God is not demanding that we give him little contributions once in a while. He was us to make a complete sacrifice and give ourselves completely and totally to Him.

CHAPTER 18

King's Friends

WELL OLD KING did it again; he couldn't resist that clover patch. The clover patch beckoned him, and even though King knew he would get sick if he ate that tasty, tender clover, he just could not resist.

Baby Doll was eyeing King as he stared longingly at the clover patch.

"King," said Baby Doll, "King, do you hear me? King, don't do it. You remember what happened last time."

But poor King had come under the spell of the clover patch. It was almost as if the clover was calling out to him, drowning out Baby Doll's warning. "Kiiiing, Kiiiiing, come over here. We are all succulently soft, warm, tasty green. Come, King, coooooome!"

As if in a trance, King slowly made his way to the clover patch despite the warnings and shouting of Baby Doll and Buddy.

That night, so it was. King's belly was twice its normal size. *Oh,* moaned King to himself, *why did I not listen to my friends? Now they will all think I am just a worthless old animal who should be put out to pasture. How can they ever be my friends again after I treated them so badly.* Poor King, disappointing his friends hurt him more than his bloated stomach.

Buddy ran and got Uncle Otto, who came out and brought his bottle of that horrid, foaming, white stuff and forced it down King's throat. Uncle Otto's mixture did its work, and by morning, King's stomach had gone down. But King was still sick. He felt his friends would never speak to him again.

Indeed, none of his friends came around but not for the reason King thought. His friends had gotten together earlier and decided that the best thing King needed was to be left alone to recover. He did not need a bunch of farm animals, sitting around clucking, snorting, mooing, baaing, or barking. So King was left alone in his misery, thinking all his friends had deserted him.

One day went by, two days, and as the animals took a quick look in the barn, they saw King lying down and not moving. Every day the animals would congregate and discuss King's condition.

"He's getting worse," mooed Baby Doll.

"But his stomach is normal," barked Buddy hopefully.

"Yeah, but he just lies there," clucked Chicken.

"Poor King," oinked Pig. "Maybe if I just slipped in and gave him a little of my slop. It always makes me feel better."

The animals discussed this and agreed that Pig could be allowed a short visit with King and share his slop, but for no more than three minutes. They did not want to disturb King in his recovery.

So Buddy gave pig his dog food bowl, and Pig filled it with slop. Pig dragged it into King.

"Here King," pleaded Pig, "This slop makes me feel better. Try it. It will help."

King looked at it and mechanically started to lap it up, while Pig stood by and watched. Oh but that slop tasted horrid, but King did not let on. He appreciated this gesture from Pig. King started to get an upset stomach from the slop, but it was a good kind of upset stomach, if you know what I mean.

Later that day, Baby Doll brought in some of her chow, Chicken brought King some of her grain, and Buddy brought a Milk Bone. All would not leave until King ate their little medicinal gifts, all of which were not horse food. But King ate them anyway, and each time his stomach raised an objection and felt sour. But it was a good kind of sour, and before long King came out of the barn, smiling and fully recovered.

All the animals gathered around King.

"King is okay. Hurrah, we have our King back," all the animals shouted.

Then Pig said, "It was my slop that healed you, wasn't it, King?"

"No," stamped Baby Doll. "It was my chow."

"Not at all," barked Buddy. "It was my Milk Bone."

The animals then started to argue with each other over whose gift healed King. Finally, King shouted, "Wait, quiet, and listen to me. It was not the food you gave me. What healed me was your friendship."

Colossians 3:16: "Let the Word of Christ dwell in you richly, teaching and encouraging one another in all wisdom, singing Psalms, hymns and spiritual songs with thankfulness in your hearts."

The best gift we can give someone is often just our time and friendship.

Chapter 19

A Taste of Honey

"YIP, YIP, YIP, yip!" howled Buddy as he ran across the farmyard.

"What's wrong with Buddy?" asked Baby Doll to King.

"He tried to rob the bee's honey again, and, of course, you know what happened," replied King.

Somehow the bees knew that it would not do much good to sting Buddy on his body. It was his nose that was most sensitive, so the bees all lined up to take their turn at giving poor Buddy a sting right on the old snout.

Owww! That hurt, and Buddy ran to the tall grass and rolled in it, trying to shake the bees away. After the bees had taken their vengeance on the hapless Buddy, he made his way to his doghouse, where he began pawing his nose as it began to swell.

"Buddy, Buddy," mooed Baby Doll with little sympathy. "Why do you do it?"

"You know those old bees will come after you if you try to rob their hive," snorted King.

"Ith thmelled tho good," said Buddy through a swollen nose.

See, dogs have a very keen sense of smell, and where you and I may not be able to smell honey, Buddy could, and when he got close enough to Uncle Otto's beehives, that sweet smell put him under a spell and he forgot all about the little guardians of the hive. All he could think of was that sweet taste of honey.

"Well Buddy," said Benjamin Goat rather self-righteously, "you know all you have to do to avoid getting your nose stung is to not go near those beehives. In that way, you will not smell the honey and then you will not be tempted to rob their hives."

Well that made all kinds of sense, but old Buddy could not resist getting near those hives just to pick up a scent of that sweet smell.

However, not too long after this incident, Uncle Otto built a chain-link fence around his beehives to keep Buddy and other animals away from them.

This was quite effective, so much so that Buddy began to brave a few trips near the hive just to pick up the scent of the honey. There would, of course, be no danger, as he could not get beyond that fence to get to the honey and risk the revengeful sting of its owners.

The trips to the hives became a daily routine for Buddy. He looked forward to passing by the hives and enjoying that rich, sweet smell of honey. Often he would pause and try to imagine drinking his fill of that rich nectar. *All I really want is just a taste of that honey,* Buddy thought. *Surely the bees would not mind me taking just a taste.*

A few days went by, and Buddy again paused before the hives, smelled the honey, and thought, *Why should the bees mind if I just take a taste of their honey? But Uncle Otto would mind. That is why he built this fence. No, I shan't disobey Uncle Otto's wishes.*

A few days later, however, Buddy stood before the hives, smelling the alluring aroma of the honey and thought. *If the bees don't mind, I am sure Uncle Otto would not mind if I just limit it to a taste.*

Not too many days later, Buddy started thinking again as he basked in the glory of that sweet delicious smell. *You know, if the bees or Uncle Otto don't mind if I have a taste of honey, I would love to have just a little taste.*

And it was only a few days later that Buddy noticed the gate was left open to the beehives. Buddy really started thinking. *I would love to have just a taste of that honey, and I am sure the bees and Uncle Otto would not mind a bit if I had just a little taste. In fact, I think the bees and Uncle Otto would have me have a taste of honey.*

With that, Buddy made his decision. He passed through the gate, went up to the beehive, and stuck his nose in the hive to get a lick of that tasty, sweet honey. Then all of a sudden—"Yip, yip, yip, yip!" Aw, Buddy's poor nose.

Jeremiah 17:9: "The heart is more deceitful than all else and is desperately sick; who can understand it?"

We must beware of temptation. If we let temptation have its way, it will eventually lead us to believe that what was once wrong is now right.

CHAPTER 20

The Pump House

Uncle Otto and King worked many days trying to remove an old stump with no success. One day Uncle Claiborne drove up in his pickup and carefully removed a couple containers. He and Uncle Otto, with great caution, mixed the contents of the containers into one container by the old stump. They moved very far away from the stump and pushed a button on a little box with wires connected to the container. There was an instant "kaboom!" and the stump was gone. Uncle Claiborne and Uncle Otto then took the kaboom stuff that they did not use and put it in the pump house and locked the door.

A week later, Uncle Otto and Aunt Ruth went on vacation, leaving their nephew Ricky to water and feed the animals every day after school. The first day Ricky laid out the feed, and all the animals gathered around to eat and drink the nice cool water. But when Ricky went to turn on the hose, no water came out.

"Oh crummy buttons," moaned Ricky. "The pump is turned off, and I need to get into the pump house to turn it on. And I don't have the key to the pump house."

All the animals followed Ricky to the pump house and watched as he played around with that piece of brass that seemed to keep the door to the pump house closed. After a while he said, "Well, I will just have to call Uncle Otto in Chicago and see where he put the key. I suppose you poor animals will have no water today."

After Ricky left, the animals gathered together for an emergency meeting.

"Oh but I am thirsty. I really need water," Benjamin Goat whimpered.

"My mouth is so dry it feels like the bottom of a haystack," bellowed King.

"My mudhole is about dried out," oinked Pig sadly. "What shall I do to keep cool in the hot sun?"

"You know," mooed Baby Doll thoughtfully, "I saw Uncle Otto push a red, little, circle thing in that pump house. The motor started, and water came out of the hose almost immediately. If we could get into that pump house, I am sure we could push that red thing and get all the water we need."

"Great idea," said King. "But how do we get in if Ricky could not get past that metal thing holding the door shut?"

"No problem," barked Buddy. "I will dig under the pump house and come up through the floor."

The animals discussed this, and all agreed that seemed right to them. So Buddy started to dig and dig and dig. Suddenly they heard a thump.

"Buddy made it," clucked Chicken hopefully.

But Buddy crawled out of his hole and wearily said, "There is a wooden floor to the house. I can't get through it."

Everyone was getting discouraged until Crow flew up and announced, "Hey gang, there is a hole in the roof of the pump house just big enough for me to crawl through and push that red thing."

The animals discussed this plan and agreed it surely was the right way to get to the water.

So Crow squeezed through hole and flew down to the pump. Baby Doll, looking through a crack in the wall of the pump house, guided Crow to the red round thing. When Crow found it, Baby Doll told him to push it real hard. Crow pecked and pecked, but he could not push it hard enough to start the pump. This plan was just not going to work.

Again the animals gathered to discuss a new plan. Benjamin Goat announced that he had the correct and proper way to get to the pump. He would put his head down and ram the door. Everyone looked at each other and agreed that this was definitely the way that seemed right to them all.

So Benjamin Goat got a running start, and running with all his might and speed, he rammed the door. The door fell off its hinges and right on top of the kaboom canisters. Suddenly, there was a loud "kaboom," and the pump house was just a pile of little sticks. Benjamin Goat, fortunately, was uninjured but was thrown into a pile of hay. The animals quickly gathered around Benjamin Goat, who stood up, shook his head, and looked at the debris that was once the pump house.

He declared, "Wow, did you see what I did? I sure can hit a door hard."

"Yeah," said Baby Doll, "and you also destroyed the pump. Now we will have no water for long time."

Benjamin Goat, however, did not care about the pump or pump house. He was just filled with great pride over his ability to reduce a little shack to rumble with one blow. Of course, we all know it was not Benjamin Goat that destroyed the pump house; it was that kaboom stuff.

> Zechariah 4:6: "Not by power, not by might, but by my Spirit says the Lord of host."

We may think we are doing something really powerful and mighty, but all the time the power and might are really from God.

Oh, and something else, that was not the way to get into the pump house.

> Proverbs 14:12: "There is a way which seems right unto a man, but the end thereof is the way of destruction."

CHAPTER 21

The Old Barn

"**W**ATCH OUT, BABY Doll!" cried King. "That loose board is about to ..."

"Bonk!" The board fell right on poor Baby Doll's head.

"Ooow! That smarts," mooed Baby Doll.

"Don't know why Uncle Otto didn't nail that board up better," mused King.

"Not Uncle Otto's fault," barked Buddy. "Those boards are just too rotted to hold a nail."

"I don't know why Uncle Otto doesn't tear this old barn down," grunted Pig.

The "old barn" was a wooden storage barn that was in the middle of the pasture and on the land when Uncle Otto purchased it. He kept water and a supply of feed for his animals in this old barn. It also provided some shelter for the animals when a sudden storm came up and they did have time to make it back to the main barn in time. It was also a nice retreat from the hot sun during any particularly warm summer day.

"I understand this barn is almost one hundred years old," clucked Chicken.

"And it hasn't had a coat of paint since," said Baby Doll.

"Nor any major repairs," said Sheep observantly.

"This is indeed one ugly, broken-down barn," oinked Pig.

"I don't know why Uncle keeps this barn up," commented Benjamin Goat as he started chewing on King's hay.

"Beats me," snorted King. "And if you don't mind, Benjamin, I would like to get to some of my hay."

"I'm sure Uncle Otto has his reasons," said Buddy as he began to lap up some cool water.

"Who can understand the ways of Uncle Otto," mooed Baby Doll as she went back to eating her chow.

"Can you look at this barn?" said King thoughtfully. "Almost one hundred years of rainstorms, hail, sleet, blizzards, wind, and hot sun. It sure has taken a beating."

"And looks it," affirmed Benjamin Goat. "That is one ugly barn, not like that beautiful new barn Uncle Otto recently built. Now that barn is nothing like this worthless old wreck."

The animals all agreed the old barn was ugly, worthless, and useless as they all walked out of its shade into the hot sun to attend to their daily routines.

A couple weeks later, Buddy ran up to the farm animals excitedly. "Hey gang, remember that old barn in the field?"

"How could I forget," mooed Baby Doll as she thought of the lump still on her head.

"Well," barked Buddy, "Harrison from the lumberyard is out there in the pasture with Uncle Otto, looking at that barn. I think they are going to tear it down."

"What did Harrison say?" asked King.

"Something about very valuable and hundreds of dollars."

"Hmm," pondered King. "Harrison must be talking about his time being valuable to use it to tear down the barn."

"And the hundreds of dollars must be what it will cost Uncle Otto to tear it down," added Benjamin Goat.

"I can't imagine why Uncle Otto would not tear it down himself and save hundreds of dollars," pondered Sheep.

"Yeah," added Chicken. "He could use that wood as firewood."

"That is about all it is worth," agreed Buddy.

"Like I said," mooed Baby Doll, "who can understand the mysterious ways of Uncle Otto."

"Uncle Otto said something else," mused Buddy thoughtfully, "He said 'donate.'"

"Who's Donate?" asked King.

"Must be someone who needs firewood," concluded Chicken.

The next day, Harrison and a crew of men arrived in a flatbed truck and carefully dismantled the old barn, put the wood on the truck, and drove off.

"Good riddance to bad rubbish, I would say." bleated Sheep.

"You know," said King sadly, "I'm going to miss that old barn. It contained some mighty good hay. I can recall how we would stop at the old barn after a hunting trip. I would be starved, and boy that hay looked and tasted so good."

"Yeah," agreed Buddy. "And I would be so thirsty, and oh how good that water in the shade of the barn was—so nice and cool."

"I remember last winter, when we had that horrible snowstorm," mused Baby Doll. "I could not make it to the new barn, but that dear, old, broken-down barn was right there in the pasture. I remember going in there to find shelter and plenty of chow."

"Me too," agreed Benjamin Goat. "I was also trapped in that storm and found shelter in the barn."

"Some days," reflected Sheep, "it would be so hot in the field, and I would find such nice cool shelter in that barn."

"Wait a minute. Wait one doggone minute," clucked Chicken

"Watch your language, Chicken," barked Buddy offended.

"Sorry, Buddy, just an expression, no offense. But come on, gang. You were just saying how ugly and useless that barn was, and now you are talking like it was something of value."

"Perhaps," said King, now quite enlightened. "Perhaps that is what Harrison meant when he said 'valuable.' For you see, it is not that ugly wooden structure that gave the barn its value. It was what was inside that barn that gave it its value."

So too with us. Maybe our outside structures are not very pretty or appear to be of little value. We may not be as beautiful, handsome, talented, or intelligent as others, but that is not what gives us our value. It is what is inside that gives us our value. For inside we can be filled with Jesus Christ, the most valuable possession in the world.

But let us return to our story and learn what happened to that old barn.

Many months had passed after the old barn was torn down when Uncle Otto took King for a ride to the Baptist church. King found everyone at the church all excited.

"What is all the excitement about?" King asked Lightning, Uncle Arthur's horse.

"Oh didn't you know?" snorted Lightning excitedly. "Today is the dedication of the new education wing of the Baptist church, and everyone is talking about the beautiful paneling in the main auditorium. They said it is the most beautiful thing they every saw. That you could not buy or manufacture wood like that anywhere. The only way to get such beautiful wood is to let it sit out in the harsh weather, with its storms, sleet, hail, blizzards, hot sun, and wind for years and years." King thought for a minute. *No, it could not be.* "Hey Lightning, do you know where they got that wood?" Lightning looked at King and said in surprise, "Why, you should know. Uncle Otto donated it. It is the wood from that old barn that was in his pasture."

Isaiah 61:3: "To appoint them that mourn in Zion, to give them beauty for ashes."

We will pass through many storms in this life, but each storm will only serve to make us more beautiful in the eyes of Jesus.

CHAIM BENTORAH IS an instructor in Hebrew for Chaim Bentorah Ministries. If you wish to contact Chaim Bentorah or the ministry with any questions or for a list of their products, please e-mail chaimbentorah@gmail.com or visit his website as www.chaimbentorah.com